A Note to Parents

DK READERS is a compelling program for beginning readers, designed in conjunction with leading literacy experts, including Dr. Linda Gambrell, Distinguished Professor of Education at Clemson University. Dr. Gambrell has served as President of the National Reading Conference, the College Reading Association, and the International Reading Association.

Beautiful illustrations and superb full-color photographs combine with engaging, easy-to-read stories to offer a fresh approach to each subject in the series. Each DK READER is guaranteed to capture a child's interest while developing his or her reading skills, general knowledge, and love of reading.

The five levels of DK READERS are aimed at different reading abilities, enabling you to choose the books that are exactly right for your child:

Pre-level 1: Learning to read
Level 1: Beginning to read
Level 2: Beginning to read alone
Level 3: Reading alone
Level 4: Proficient readers

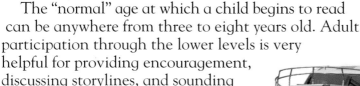

P9-ELR-534

The "normal" age at which a child begins to read can be anywhere from three to eight years old. Adult participation through the lower levels is very helpful for providing encouragement, discussing storylines, and sounding out unfamiliar words.

No matter which level you select, you can be sure that you are helping your child learn to read, then read to learn!

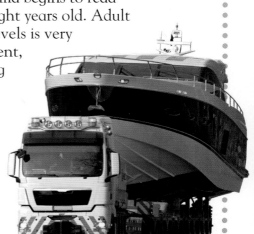

LONDON, NEW YORK, MUNICH,
MELBOURNE, AND DELHI

DK LONDON
Series Editor Deborah Lock
Art Director Martin Wilson
Production Editor Francesca Wardell
Jacket Designer Martin Wilson
Reading Consultant
Linda Gambrell, Ph.D

DK DELHI
Senior Editor Priyanka Nath
Senior Art Editor Rajnish Kashyap
Assistant Editor Deeksha Saikia
Assistant Designer Tanvi Sahu
DTP Designer Anita Yadav
Picture Researcher Sumedha Chopra

First American Edition, 2013
Published in the United States by DK Publishing
375 Hudson Street, New York, New York 10014

13 14 15 16 17 10 9 8 7 6 5 4 3 2 1
001—187464—June/2013

DK books are available at special discounts when purchased in bulk for sales
promotions, premiums, fund-raising, or educational use.

For details, contact: DK Publishing Special Markets
375 Hudson Street, New York, New York 10014
SpecialSales@dk.com

A catalog record for this book is available from the Library of Congress.

ISBN: 978-1-46540-890-7 (Paperback)
ISBN: 978-1-46540-891-4 (Hardcover)

Color reproduction by Colourscan, Singapore
Printed and bound in China by L Rex Printing Co., Ltd.

The publisher would like to thank the following for their kind
permission to reproduce their photographs:
a=above, b=below/bottom, c=center, l=left, r=right, t=top

4 Getty Images: Jetta Productions / Iconica (b). 5 Corbis: Dave Blackey / All
Canada Photos. 6 Corbis: Federico Gambarini / dpa (bl). Dreamstime.com:
Anhong (br). 7 Getty Images: Dieter Spears / Photodisc (bl). 8-9 Alamy Images:
Wally Bauman Photo. 8 Dreamstime.com: Jaypetersen (br). 9 Corbis: Ken
Davies (br). Dreamstime.com: Blaze86 (bl). 10-11 Alamy Images: Manfred Bail
/ imagebroker. 11 Alamy Images: format4 (br); Andrew Rubtsov (t). Getty
Images: Thinkstock / Comstock Images (bl). 12-13 Corbis: Nick Rains. 12
Dreamstime.com: David Gaylor (bl). 13 Dreamstime.com: Michael Shake (bc);
Thyrymn (br). Shutterstock: (bl). 14-15 Corbis: Stangot. 14
Dreamstime.com: Stepan Olenych (bl, br). 15 Dreamstime.com: Stepan
Olenych (bl); Steirus (br). 16 Dreamstime.com: Rui Matos (bl); Philippa Willitts
(br). Getty Images: Bloomberg (c). 17 Corbis: HBSS. Dreamstime.com: Artzzz
(bl); Christian Lagereek (bc). Getty Images: Stockbyte (br). 18-19 Dreamstime.
com: Picstudio. 19 Dreamstime.com: Grafvision (br); Photobac (bl). Fotolia:
skampixel (tr). Getty Images: Vasiliki Varvaki / Photodisc (bc). 20 Dreamstime.
com: Dmitry Kalinovsky (bl). 21 Dreamstime.com: Dmitry Kalinovsky (bc).
22-23 Corbis: Naljah Feanny. 23 Dreamstime.com: Mlan61 (bl). 24-25 Getty
Images: John Macdougall / AFP. 24 Dreamstime.com: Reinhardt (bl). 25
Dreamstime.com: Bjorn Heller (bc); Dmitri Melnik (br). 26-27 Corbis:
moodboard. 26 Dreamstime.com: Dtfoxfoto (bl). Getty Images: Universal
Images Group (br). 27 Dreamstime.com: Ralf Broskvar (bc, tr); Robert Pernell
(bl). Getty Images: Robert Llewellyn / Workbook Stock (br). 28-29 Alamy
Images: Marvin Dembinsky Photo Associates. 28 Dreamstime.com: Robwilson39
(br). 29 Dorling Kindersley: Aberdeen Fire Department, Maryland (bl).
Dreamstime.com: Robwilson39 (bc); Charles Vazquez (br). 30-31 Corbis: Alan
Ashley / NewSport. 30 Corbis: Car Culture (br). 31 Dreamstime.com: Gorgios
(bc); Gunter Nezhoda (bl). 33 Corbis: Federico Gambarini / dpa (br)

Jacket images: Front: Corbis: Mark Karrass

All other images © Dorling Kindersley
For further information see: www.dkimages.com

Discover more at
www.dk.com

Contents

DK READERS

LEARNING
pre-level **1** TO READ

Big Trucks

DK

DK Publishing

Trucks are BIG.

Trucks are heavy.

Trucks pull and carry loads.

The truck carries goods along the road.

goods

trucks

cab

The flatbed truck carries loads on its trailer.

trailer

flatbed trucks

load

The tow truck carries a broken-down car.

boom ——

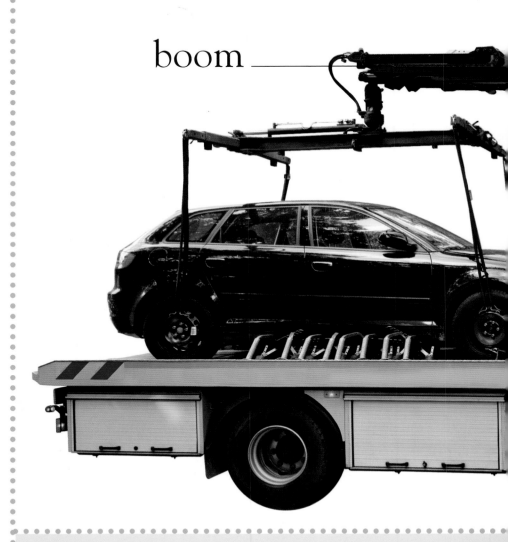

tow trucks

tow
hitch

exhaust

big rigs

The big rig pulls many trailers on long trips.

trailer

The heavy road roller flattens the road.

road rollers

drum roller

The forklift truck moves the loads.

load

 forklift trucks

driver

fork

The digger will lift the rubble in its bucket.

bucket

diggers

rubble

The wheel loader scoops up large rocks.

wheel loaders

bucket

rock

The dump truck
tips up its back so
the rubble slides out.

open-box bed

dump trucks

cab

The excavator
digs trenches with
its shovel.

excavators

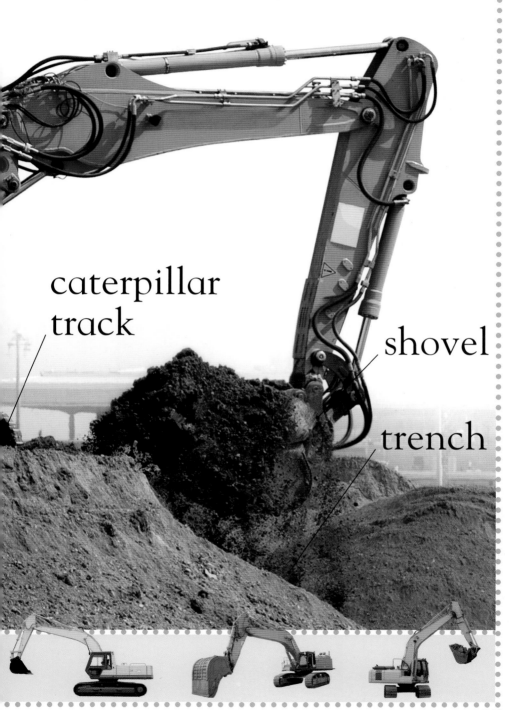

caterpillar track

shovel

trench

The compactor
presses down with
its spiked wheels.

compactors

spiked
wheel

The fire trucks have hoses and ladders to help put out fires.

ladder _____.

fire trucks

_____ hose

The monster truck does stunts on its huge wheels.

monster trucks

hood

wheel

Glossary

Compactor
a machine that squashes waste or soil into smaller amounts

Excavator
a machine that has a cab and bucket on a turning platform

Forklift truck
a truck that lifts and moves loads

Monster truck
a pickup truck with very large wheels for doing stunts

Wheel loader
a machine with a bucket to dig out earth and rocks